An Analysis of the Lord of Shadows

An Analysis of the Lord of Shadows

A
FRANDSENFILES
REPORT

Dakota Frandsen

Revitalized Occult and Strange

Contents

ISBN: 979-8-8692-7107-5 (Print)
EISBN: 979-8-8692-7108-2 (Ebook)

Disclaimer:

Exploration of supernatural claims should be approached with respect and caution. The experiences and analyses presented in this book are based on the author's research and expertise; however, they may not reflect universal truths or scientific consensus.

The entity described in this book is long documented to cause physical harm and death in reported encounters. Readers are strongly advised against attempting to confront the being in question or engaging with any affiliated phenomenon without proper training, supervision, and precautionary measures.

By reading this book, the reader acknowledges and agrees that they assume all responsibility for any actions or consequences that may result from their interpretation or application of the information provided herein. The author, publisher, and Bald and Bonkers Network LLC disclaim any liability for direct, indirect, incidental, or consequential damages arising from the use of this book.

Meet the Author

Dakota Frandsen is a name synonymous with the unexplained and the extraordinary. As the Specialist of the Strange, Frandsen has dedicated his life to unraveling the mysteries that lie beyond the realm of ordinary perception. His multifaceted career encompasses a range of roles, each contributing to his unique expertise in the world of the paranormal.

As a Paranormal Investigator, Frandsen has delved into countless cases of supernatural phenomena, from apparitions and poltergeists to cryptids and extraterrestrial encounters. His meticulous attention to detail and unwavering determination have led to the discovery of hidden truths and the debunking of myths.

In his capacity as an Exorcist, Frandsen has confronted entities that defy conventional explanation. His mastery of spiritual warfare and his deep understanding of occult practices have made him a formidable adversary to malevolent forces that seek to disrupt the natural order.

Not content with merely investigating and confronting the unknown, Frandsen is also an accomplished Author, sharing his knowledge and experiences with a global audience. His writings, including the acclaimed "FrandsenFiles," serve as a beacon of guidance for those who seek answers in the shadows.

Beyond his individual endeavors, Frandsen is the visionary CEO of Bald and Bonkers Network LLC, a platform dedicated to exploring the fringe realms of existence. Under his leadership, the network has become a hub for seekers of truth and a catalyst for groundbreaking discoveries.

As the Host of the Bald and Bonkers Show, a bi-weekly podcast that delves into various events and phenomena, Frandsen brings his expertise to the forefront, engaging with experts, witnesses, and skeptics alike to shed light on the unexplained.

FrandsenFiles, a comprehensive media collection comprising videos, books, and music, stands as a testament to Frandsen's tireless efforts to document and understand the supernatural. Through this repository of knowledge, he offers assistance to people across the globe, empowering them to navigate the mysteries that surround us.

The purpose of Frandsen's latest endeavor, "An Analysis of the Lord of Shadows: A FrandsenFiles Report," is nothing short of groundbreaking. This moniker, given to a well-known and documented "shadow being" that has terrorized individuals worldwide, represents a culmination of Frandsen's investigations and battles against this malevolent entity. In this report, Frandsen unveils his deep insights into the Lord of Shadows, revealing a perfect counterattack crafted by him and surprising allies against a being that may have inspired one of the four horsemen of the apocalypse.

Dakota Frandsen's relentless pursuit of truth and his unwavering dedication to understanding the enigmatic make him a figure of reverence and admiration in the realm of the strange and the supernatural.

Summary

Entity:

Lord of Shadows (or LOS)

Location:

Global

Classification:

Dangerous Intelligent Entity

Possible Nephilim

Potentially Godlike

WARNING:

This entity has shown the potential to cause significant harm or even death. Those who feel they may not be in the best state of mind should probably avoid reading this text in detail as it may make you a susceptible target. LOS is highly intelligent, most likely older than nearly every religious practice known to man, and has proven itself to be capable of almost every alleged form of spiritual attack.

Personal information involving various individuals will be mentioned in this report for simple documentation and reference purposes only. This information has been shared by the individuals in question and is NOT by any means meant to discriminate against any of them. For the safety of civilians outside of the company, and who haven't established a public appearance, names have been altered.

Summary:

First identified *-redacted-* is an entity that visits countless people seemingly around times of personal trauma. Most eyewitnesses report he appears in times of poor mental health, domestic violence, and drug use. Often he is stated to appear in the bed of night in his intended target's bedroom and just watches. He has also been known to show up at locations of significant tragedy that may respond to the circumstances mentioned above. It seems most common that individuals report visitations from this entity right around puberty.

-redacted- has also published two books regarding the entity, shadow people in general, and how to deal with them. Her publication company and herself have also trademarked the terms *-redacted-* allegedly as an effort to throttle misinformation to prevent further injury to potential victims.

Personal Encounter:

I know not how long this entity has had its eye on me. The earliest I can account for something similar to its presence was roughly at the age of three. This was after my life was almost taken by my stepmother, but I could fight back. At the age of fourteen, I had learned my father was being charged for sexually assaulting one of my sisters; and it prompted another visit from this thing. Only this time, it spoke, offering me a deal to join him in return for the death of my father. As for what, I don't know. Other voices that came through pierced my own as I yelled for it to get away, and it seemed to deter it. Other times when it appeared circumstances were surrounding further domestic violence, suicidal tendencies, violent and psychotic episodes, etc...

For location reference - the incident involving the knife and my stepmother took place in November 1999. In 2002, I somehow transported 30 miles away from home. Thankfully the location I turned up was my grandparent's house, likely in response to possible trauma (psychic teleportation or alien abduction has been suggested). When I learned of the charges against my father and the subsequent deal, it was June of 2012.

Preliminary

Preliminary Investigation:

Apart from *-redacted-* book, limited information existed regarding this entity and its motivations beyond the unsettling experiences reported by numerous witnesses. Due to this recurring pattern, the official investigation, led by the "Specialist of the Strange" among other titles, was temporarily suspended pending further developments. The standard protocol involved guiding clients towards overcoming potential traumas that could trigger encounters with the LOS, with the expectation that over time, its power and influence would wane. Despite the air of mystery surrounding this entity, it appeared relatively harmless, deriving joy from misfortunes that may invite its presence. References to the LOS and related phenomena were cautioned as potential triggers for further disturbances.

A Turning Point:

For years, I set aside the investigation into this entity as no significant breakthroughs surfaced. However, during a casual conversation with my ex-partner, Jane, she recounted her chilling encounter with the LOS. What made her experience noteworthy was a deviation in the entity's behavior. While visiting a former boyfriend in the summer of 2015, Jane described an incident where a bathroom door slammed shut and remained held, coinciding with a shadowy figure resembling the LOS brandishing a knife and charging at her former partner. Unsurprisingly, their relationship didn't last much longer after that ordeal.

Jane fit the victimology criteria associated with the LOS, displaying signs of childhood trauma and strained familial relationships, leading to fragmented memories from severe abuse during her childhood. Unfortunately, this trauma often manifested in her choice of abusive relationships, possibly unconsciously echoing past experiences. Although Jane never fully disclosed the extent of her past to me, she expressed feeling triggered by

scenes resembling a "kill room" from the Show-
time TV series *"Dexter."*

This encounter reignited my interest in the
phenomenon, as any deviations in behavior could
offer valuable insights. Comparing Jane's account
to others revealed minimal changes in the LOS's
modus operandi. However, a distinct pattern
emerged, particularly concerning episodes of sleep
paralysis. Witnesses reported seeing a tall, slender
shadow looming over them either before falling
asleep or upon waking abruptly from a deep slum-
ber but not fully conscious. It's important to note
that these visions align with hypnagogic or hyp-
nopompic experiences, where dream-like visuals
persist upon awakening.

For those unfamiliar with hypnagogia or
hypnopompia, these terms describe a state where
dream visuals blend with waking reality, akin
to augmented reality for those familiar with the
concept. Such states are often triggered by stress,
raising the possibility of the LOS's presence coinciding with heightened mental states, even if it's

not a genuine encounter but rather a manifestation of an overwhelmed mind.

Plague

The chaos of the COVID-19 pandemic, particularly in 2020, marked a significant shift in our investigation. Seeking more insights, I turned to Reddit and asked for narratives related to the LOS. An anonymous user directed me to Breton mythology, where variations of the Grim Reaper or Death's servant are depicted as the Ankou. Like many mythological figures, the Ankou's portrayal varies across regions.

The Ankou is sometimes depicted as a man or skeleton wearing a black robe and a large hat concealing his face. Other times, he manifests as a shadow apparition. One story posits that the Ankou is the last person, typically male, to die in the preceding year. Another suggests multiple Ankou existing simultaneously, each confined to specific regions. Particularly intriguing is the tale linking the Ankou to Cain, Adam and Eve's first-born son and infamous for fratricide.

This revelation prompted deeper exploration into the events within the Garden of Eden that triggered Cain's murderous act. It was crucial to avoid fixating on a single religious text and instead analyze various accounts to discern any potential connection between the Hatman and humanity's origins. Within Jewish lore, details about the serpent in the Garden of Eden piqued interest.

While many associate the serpent with Lucifer, this assumption may be erroneous. Lucifer is indeed categorized as a fallen angel, but contrary to popular belief, he is not synonymous with "Satan" in its modern sense. Examining Hebrew translations of various texts reveals that "Satan" was originally used as a verb, denoting an adversary. The term "Ha Satan" when prefixed with "Ha," serves as a noun or title. Early Judeo-Christian texts mention only one entity directly referred to as "Satan" – Samael, an archangel associated with Death and speculated to be Cain's biological father.

Two weeks later, I received a call on my professional hotline just as I was returning home from work. The call pertained to a family from North Carolina, and from the outset, the overall tone of the conversation hinted at a potentially sinister situation. Driven by my ethical responsibilities, I delved deeper into the matter. The client expressed concerns about an entity seemingly directing its attention towards his three-year-old son.

Our conversation spanned approximately three hours as we established rapport and trust. During this time, the client shared numerous signs indicative of demonic influences, including unusual odors, deep scratches, and objects being moved without explanation – all classic symptoms. The client described encounters where an entity resembling the Hatman engaged him in conversations aligned with his interests. Notably, objects would seemingly be thrown when the entity was spoken ill of, serving as warnings.

Furthermore, the client mentioned a specific room in their house, referred to as the "Dead Room," which appeared to cause physical discomfort upon entry. He recounted an incident where the entity physically assaulted him in a public setting, adding to the gravity of the situation. Meanwhile, as the client moved about his house during our call, a secondary voice resembling that of a child emerged, coinciding with the wife's prior miscarriage.

The husband's description of the voice suggested a child between five to seven years old, a detail possibly connected to the miscarriage experience. It's not uncommon for miscarried children to be believed to visit their intended parents. The alarming statement made by the alleged child during the call underscored the need for further investigation.

The child stated, "Put down the fucking phone or I'll kill you bitch."

During our discussions, I inquired about the entity's self-identification, a crucial step in building trust and understanding. The entity, identifying itself as "Cain," purportedly sought to recruit the husband with promises of leadership within its "army."

In response to these distressing events, I provided the family with a protective sigil crafted with possible guidance from the archangel Michael. This sigil had previously been effective in resolving similar cases involving malevolent entities, including one notable instance in Pittsburgh that garnered attention from *-redacted-*. The father's past experimentation with DMT, a substance believed by some to have spiritual connections, and the son's early sensitivity to paranormal elements were also noted, though it's anticipated that the latter will naturally wane over time pending other outside stimuli do not factor in.

Several days following the intense encounter with the distressed family in North Carolina, a remarkable and otherworldly event unfolded within the confines of my own bedroom. An enigmatic figure materialized before me, standing at an approximate height of five feet. It cloaked itself within a swirling veil of shadow, yet subtle hints of feminine curves were perceptible amidst the obscurity. The figure's eyes, radiant with an otherworldly light, emerged first from the shroud, accompanied by a gentle, inviting smile. As the figure gradually revealed more of its form, I discerned features reminiscent of Middle Eastern descent: sparkling brown eyes, olive-toned skin, and a cascade of curly black hair. When I inquired about her identity, she responded with cryptic grace, stating, "I've been known by many names, but you recognize me as Eve."

Eve's presence transcended mere physicality; she exuded an aura of ancient wisdom and profound significance. Placing her hand upon my temple, she initiated a transcendent experience, channeling visions that seemed to transport me to the mythic Garden of Eden itself. The surroundings felt eerily familiar, as if I had walked its sacred grounds in a past life. Through Eve's guidance, I was granted insight into her tumultuous relationship with Samael, the mistreatment she endured from Adam, and the consequential impact on Cain, whose festering resentment and anguish ultimately led to the tragic fratricide of Abel.

The vividness of the vision was hauntingly real; I witnessed the pivotal moment of Cain's murderous act against his brother. Abel's defiant blow, striking Cain's face with a rock, only fueled Cain's rage further, marking the genesis of what would later possibly be known as the "Mark of Cain." Intriguingly, there are reported sightings linking this ancient tale to the modern phenomenon of the LOS, with mentions of possible scar tissue on the right side of the figure's face, akin to Cain's biblical mark. I cannot help but speculate that this "mark" was meant to serve as a reminder of the psychological turmoil, and inevitable prison of mind, of knowing that his hands were now stained by the blood of his brother.

When the vision dissipated, I inquired with Eve about her reasons for revealing these images. Her reply was that aspects of me reminded her of what Cain could have become and that is what made me dangerous to someone like him. The love she had for her sons was consuming her, I could feel the guilt she carried for not being able to do more. She also referenced our mutual bloodline, something

I would not understand the full meaning of until years later, bound us all forever.

In a separate yet equally intriguing development, a distressed woman reached out to me following my online inquiries regarding the LOS phenomenon. Upon learning about my dedicated podcast episode on the subject, she urgently sought to listen to it before engaging further. Her subsequent communication revealed a chilling reality: she had been visited by an entity around the time of her 5-month-old son's birth, a presence that unnervingly fixated on the infant. However, her trepidation escalated upon discovering the entity's alleged identity as Cain, the very name she had bestowed upon her child.

To safeguard against further encounters, the protective sigil I had devised was administered, offering a semblance of protection and tranquility. Since then, she has reported no additional encounters with the entity, finding solace in the warding properties of the sigil. These interconnected experiences serve as profound glimpses into the intricate web of supernatural phenomena and human consciousness, weaving ancient myths with contemporary mysteries in a tapestry of enigmatic significance.

The Attack

Ambushed:

Through my social media management platform, I strategically disseminated notifications across various digital channels, aiming to curate a reservoir of narratives conducive to crafting a comprehensive documentary delving beyond the prevailing "he's simply evil" trope enveloping the ongoing discourse. Under the banner of *-redacted-*, an international initiative was set in motion to amass a trove of insights into the enigmatic entity known as LOS. Initial efforts included reaching out to -redacted- for direct dialogue; however, legal constraints stemming from her trademarked term impeded further discourse. *-redacted-*

Undeterred by these constraints, our investigation pivoted toward establishing a chronological framework delineating the spatial-temporal occurrences of LOS manifestations, alongside meticulously cataloging comprehensive eyewitness testimonies. Admittedly, there lingered skepticism regarding the efficacy of this approach, given its heavy reliance on narratives steeped in profound psychological trauma, often muddled by the mind's instinctual defense mechanisms. Nevertheless, it constituted the most viable foundation for our investigative trajectory.

The subsequent phase witnessed an influx of anecdotal submissions primarily sourced from Reddit and mirrored across our social media platforms. While seemingly expedient, this methodological simplicity was marred by inherent vulnerabilities, as elucidated by the orchestrated assaults that besieged the *-redacted-* YouTube Channel on February 12th and 13th. These meticulously coordinated attacks on the 13th resulted in a cascade of disruptions, culminating in the possession of panelist *-redacted-*, who was promptly subjected to an on-air exorcism helmed by myself, effectively prompting the cessation of our formal investigation.

The aftermath was characterized by an unprecedented deluge of psychological distress within our team's ranks. *-redacted-* grappling with overwhelming personal circumstances, necessitated an extended hiatus to prioritize mental well-being. A subsequent analysis of audio recordings from the tumultuous live streams unearthed unsettling directives such as "Quit hunting us" and "Tear him apart," alongside explicit targeting of specific members, namely *-redacted-*. These distressing revelations underscored the potential multi-dimensional nature of the entities involved, blurring the lines between malevolence and attempted assistance.

Moreover, *-redacted-* account of being left under the purported supervision of entities affiliated with LOS during the onslaught warrants cautious scrutiny, given her adversarial demeanor following the ordeal. Regrettably, prudence dictates treating these claims with circumspection, redirecting our resources toward extending support to other potential victims.

A notable incident involving *-redacted-*, though not directly involved in the panel, attests to the indiscriminate nature of LOS's influence. Her encounter during a Reiki protection endeavor resulted in minor repercussions akin to a mild sunburn, prompting swift disengagement to safeguard both herself and her young children from potential harm.

War

Amidst the Shadows:

I harbored an intuitive sense that LOS would not simply vanish from our sphere of concern. This entity possessed an unnerving ability to traverse realms, perceiving its victims at the minutest levels, from internal physiological movements to the innermost recesses of their minds. I delved deeper into the investigation, collating a myriad of encounter reports, each unveiling increasingly disconcerting patterns.

One narrative involved a young man consumed by vengeance following the demise of his father and best friend, attributing their deaths to the entity. Another poignant account stemmed from a distressed mother whose three-year-old daughter often vocally repelled an unseen entity she termed as the "shadow man," moments before experiencing an inexplicable fall down the stairs. Additionally, a woman recounted harrowing encounters with shadowy apparitions, indicative of a pervasive presence.

Out of respect for *-redacted-* need for emotional convalescence post-encounter, minimal contact was maintained. Still grappling with residual trauma, *-redacted-* expunged all LOS-related records from *-redacted-* systems, aiming to prevent inadvertent provocation of further disruptions.

Whether fortuitous or tethered by a psychic thread, a few weeks later witnessed concerted efforts to sever the dark energies enveloping *-redacted-*. Occult methodologies were harnessed to sever connections, commencing with Shannon's account of residual entities left behind by LOS. An attempt was made to broker a deal with LOS, offering an alternative avenue for its malevolent activities in exchange for ceasing intrusions on *-redacted-*. This strategic maneuver aimed to buy time for orchestrating a potent counter-strategy, rendering LOS impotent outside its putative role akin to the Grim Reaper. Remarkably, within hours of initiating these negotiations, *-redacted-*

reported the vanishing of entities. Curiously, discussions among the entities referenced "the Knowing One," prompting *-redacted-* speculation that it referred to my involvement.

An intriguing proposal posited by *-redacted-* entailed crafting an "Anti-LOS" entity using occult practices to thwart potential attacks. Thus, a sigil was conceived, birthing the "Knight of Light," imbued with energies from the archangel Michael to counteract potential satanic influences. Remarkably, within weeks of circulating this sigil, a mother reported her daughter's exclamation of being rescued by the "Knight Light." Equally intriguing was the child's subsequent excitement upon recognizing me during a video call, referring to me as the "Knight."

Simultaneously, *-redacted-* exhibited gradual recovery, resuming active participation within our endeavors. Notably, sightings of a shadowy figure trailing *-redacted-* experiences, prompted speculation of a shared observer phenomenon. Months later, during an informal discussion, *-redacted-* mention of angels led to a recollection of my

encounter with a girl named *Olivia,* which res-
onated with *-redacted-* recurring dreams featuring a similar figure. This serendipitous alignment
spurred further investigation.

A striking revelation emerged when a baby picture resembling *Olivia* surfaced, inciting *-redacted-*
emotional reaction. Subsequent discoveries, including a picture featuring myself alongside twin
girls (younger cousins of mine) resembling *Olivia*
at a young age, reinforced the veracity of *-redacted-*
experiences. The notion that *Olivia's* visibility was
restricted to blood ties was dispelled, especially
considering *-redacted-* similar genetic heritage to
my own and shared sighting experiences. This
revelation broadened the scope of our inquiry,
hinting at intricate connections transcending familial boundaries.

-redacted- provided invaluable insights into the
LOS investigation. She was the sole member who
disclosed prior encounters with the entity, detailing physical assaults that began when she was
around fourteen years old. *-redacted-* recounted

recurring nightmares where she found herself engulfed in darkness, confronted by LOS's unsettling visage looming above her. These nightmares, she believed, were interconnected and echoed feelings of isolation during times of distress, possibly stemming from insecurities about self-worth in relationships. Subsequently, following the attacks, *-redacted-* took a hiatus from *-redacted-* to address mental health challenges. Out of respect for her privacy and the focus of our inquiry, specific details regarding her struggles are omitted.

Remarkably, I experienced a dream mirroring Ashley's recurring nightmares, featuring LOS's presence in darkness. However, in this dream, I intervened, confronting the entity from behind. The subsequent days, *-redacted-* exhibited increased engagement with our team. Upon conversing, *-redacted-* and I unearthed striking parallels in our backgrounds—we were born in consecutive months in 1995 and 1996, shared comparable astrological profiles, psychic sensitivities, and genetic lineages. Notably, we both had affiliations with potent entities often perceived as opposing forces. Further investigation using ley line mapping revealed that we resided equidistant from a minor ley line, potentially facilitating communication via the Necrophonic app and facilitating *Olivia's* appearances between us.

Collaborating with *-redacted-*, I compiled enough data to generate an image of *Olivia* using age progression techniques employed in missing children cases. During podcast recordings, they captured an EVP featuring a childlike voice saying "Ding dong" and a faint "Mommy," fueling speculation that Ashley might be Olivia's biological mother. However, subsequent information contradicted this hypothesis, suggesting Olivia wasn't traveling alone. *-redacted-* likeness was utilized in rendering *Olivia's* image, later confirmed to be an exact match by *-reducted-* herself.

This revelation raised two intriguing possibilities. Firstly, *Olivia* might have been accompanied and guided by someone referred to as "mommy." Reports from individuals sensitive to paranormal energies described sensing *Olivia* holding someone's hand, although no visible figure accompanied her.

The second possibility, which still carries some weight, suggests that Ashley bore a physical resemblance to Olivia's actual mother, and Olivia herself may have had vision impairments. To further explore the connection between *-redacted-* and me, *-redacted-* an urgent message with the opening words, "Call Dakota, I think I just saw *Olivia*." *-redacted-* had previously mentioned spotting a young girl with blonde hair around his vicinity, even before meeting me, indicating that *Olivia* may have been watching over specific individuals for an extended period in addition to visiting me.

The emergency message conveyed an SOS, detailing *-redacted-* encounter with *Olivia* just before he was reportedly attacked and potentially influenced by a shadow entity. Upon considering the possibility of possession, *-redacted-* and I embarked on a remote exorcism to sever the connection between *-redacted-* and the entity. I monitored the situation using Necrophonic, which signaled when the link to *-redacted-* was severed, prompting him to contact *-redacted-* and me. During our conversation, *-redacted-* revealed that he had felt compelled to avoid the phone at all costs, sensing a growing anger whenever he thought of reaching out to me, specifically, for assistance. When shown the rendered image of Olivia, *-redacted-*confirmed that he hadn't gotten a clear view of her face during the encounter.

Reinforcements

"Daddy's Girl... from Beyond?":

Olivia's presence in my life traces back to when I was around twelve years old, although recent events hint that she might have been around even longer. The potential involvement of time-travel further complicates establishing a precise timeline. Olivia would manifest unpredictably whenever I found myself in a dark mental space, offering words of encouragement. On three notable occasions, she appeared either to forewarn me of impending deaths, provide solace, or caution me of impending dangers.

The second encounter occurred on the day of my maternal grandfather's passing due to cancer. Olivia appeared and offered to share her vision, allowing me to witness my grandfather's final moments through astral travel. While I couldn't be physically present in the room due to responsibilities as the eldest sibling, Olivia's presence was perceptible to my grandfather during his final hours.

The third incident took place in October 2014 during a car accident where I was struck by a pickup truck traveling at 60 mph. The impact knocked me unconscious, but I firmly believe Olivia appeared moments before the collision, urgently warning, "Daddy! Look out!"

The fourth significant encounter happened in April 2016 while I was in Paris, France. During a riverboat cruise to admire the Eiffel Tower's light show, a sudden rainstorm forced others to seek shelter below deck. However, I remained on deck until a tap on my shoulder diverted my attention. To my astonishment, I saw my grandfather and Olivia standing beside me. They conveyed that their visits would become less frequent as I no longer required as much guidance. Despite this, EVP recordings from various cases indicate that my grandfather sporadically checks in to observe my endeavors. Had Olivia ceased her appearances, this report would have been considerably shorter.

Over time, I came to understand that both Olivia and my grandfather were trying to provide support and encouragement to keep me moving forward. However, the increased activity of Olivia remains a subject of speculation. Upon joining Parachills, I produced two films for the streaming network Paraflixx. One was titled "The Hunt for Olivia," delving deeper into what I termed the Olivia Paradox. The other film, "Bonds of Beyond," aimed to explore the intersection between the ET/ UFO phenomenon and spiritual phenomena. It's worth noting that an earlier project, "The Hunt for Infinite Earths," inspired the development of "Bonds of Beyond." Through these projects, several entities emerged with potential interest:

- Michael the Archangel

- Gabriel the Archangel

- Metatron

- Yeshuah (also known as Jesus, translating directly to Joshua)

- Yahweh

- El

- Ashtar

- Vrillon

- Athena

- John *-redacted-* (referred to as John in "Bonds of Beyond," a DC Comics/Vertigo character based on real occult information; some claim to have interacted with him in our world)
- Aleister Crowley (communications were attempted via spirit box to gather information about the Hatman, and he has purportedly offered assistance in the fight against it)

Through interactions with *-redacted-*, two additional entities came into focus:
- Lucifer
- Lilith

-redacted- provided insights into more entities worth studying, believed to be connected to the Pleiadians:
- Artemis/Diana
- Apollo

UFO contact experiments were also conducted, focusing on members of the "Ashtar Command," which resulted in intriguing video footage of strange objects appearing. Whenever attention was directed towards "Ashtar's crew," *Olivia* would manifest. Additionally, I had a dream where I found myself in a futuristic hospital room where a woman lay in bed holding a baby boy. *Olivia* sat beside her and introduced the baby as her brother, calling me "Daddy." Upon waking, the word "Tachyonis" emerged from my thoughts. A quick search revealed it as a theoretical particle associated with time travel, claimed by some new-age groups to enable Pleiadians' space travel.

The following day, **-redacted-**, a psychic medium known as **-redacted-**, mentioned the need to discuss my experience. During a "mini-reading," *Olivia's* voice came through the speaker, further contributing to the understanding of *Olivia's* potential mother and her grown baby brother.

Victim Profiles

Known and Alleged Victims:

Below is a list of known victims that have come forward in regards the "Hatman" phenomenon. Also noted are events which showcase the psychological profiles of each subject to be noted simply for observation. This is to recap all previous information plus add more potentially necessary information.

Below is a list of known victims that have come forward in regards the "LOS" phenomenon. Also noted are events which showcase the psychological profiles of each subject to be noted simply for observation. This is to recap all previous information plus add more potentially necessary information.

-redacted- Members

Dakota Frandsen:

- History of anger management
  - Violent outbursts have occurred to where police had to get involved out of concern of the safety of others involved
    - This was primarily because Dakota physically developed rather quickly as a child, causing him to grow to be 6'7" and over 300lbs
    - Physical altercations were common as well due to Dakota being bullied at school
    - One incident, while Dakota was the age of three, involved him stabbing his stepmother in the abdomen
      - She had attacked Dakota first by stabbing him with a ballpoint pen, which he then fought back
- Grew up in abusive family dynamic
  - Father who was physically, mentally, and sexually abusive to nearly all he knew
    - Father is *-redacted-* Frandsen,

who is currently serving time for the sexual abuse of one of Dakota's younger sisters

- *-redacted-* spent time in the foster system, likely abused at a young age himself
- Rumors of an incestuous relationship took place between *-redacted-*
- Has history of illegal substance abuse
- Many of *-redacted-* children, even ones who were miscarried, may have been conceived under sexual assault
- The sexual assaults on Dakota's younger sister showed signs of a child being conceived, however the pregnancy terminated itself
  - Dakota's sister was age 12
- It is unknown if, though incredibly likely, *-redacted-* had encountered LOS before

- Mother is *-redacted-* who has had severe tendencies to allow herself to become emotionally unstable
  - Frequently assaulted Dakota, threatening to pin the blame on him if he tried to retaliate because of his stature
  - Constantly compared Dakota to his father, even after his father's history of sexual assaults cam to light
- Tends to work alone, even on dangerous projects, because of trust issues
- Dakota has been noted to potentially have a direct connection to the archangel Michael
  - Attempted suicide at the age of twelve
    - Allegedly an encounter/vision saved his life
      - In this incident, Dakota saw himself in a blue void
      - While in this void a man approached Dakota, whose image seemed blurry
        - Dakota was able to make out roughly

shoulder-length, dirty blonde or brown hair
  ○ Also wearing what appeared to be a white robe
• Man approached Dakota, with calm but concerned energies from him
• Man smiles reveals to Dakota a little girl who resembles him
• Little girl claims Dakota is her father
  ○ May have extraterrestrial connection
    ■ Needs further study
• Man was identified by various sources to potentially be Michael the Archangel
• Has family history of psychic ability
  ○ Ranges from magic manipulation, weather manipulation telekinesis, clairvoyance, mediumship
  ○ Speculated to either have accidentally

teleported or was intercepted by extraterrestrials at the age of five

- ■ This was an incident where Dakota somehow ended up roughly 30 miles away from the house he went to bed

    - He appeared the next morning at the home of his maternal grandparents, *-redacted-*

        - *-redacted-* to this day had no clue how Dakota got into the house, or that he was even there

        - *-redacted-* passed when Dakota was 15 due to complications with cancer

            ○ It should be noted that *-redacted-*, in his final moments, acted as if he could see a young girl matching Dakota's alleged daughter

            ○ *-redacted-* still

appears via EVP sessions, likely travels with Dakota

  ◦ Dakota spotted *-redacted-* with the little girl while on a trip to Paris

  ◦ *-redacted-* allegedly confirms that it was the little girl he saw, and that Dakota was in fact abducted by extraterrestrials

  • *-redacted-* called grandparents the next morning fearing Dakota had been kidnapped

• Father was absent from picture, highly unlikely he would have left Dakota at that location if this was a case of parental kidnapping

• Also suffered a serious head blow as a baby from *-redacted-* throwing him into the ceiling

• Been in and out of hospital due to medical issues as a child

- Has had at least three near-death-experiences as of January 2022
    - Recounts meeting deceased relatives, a woman identifying herself as Eve, Michael the archangel
- Looks to experiment more with potential methods to artificially enhance psychic potential
- May have had sexual relations with an extra-terrestrial which resulted in two hybrid children
    - The little girl, Olivia Hope, has shown psychic potential
        - May be guided by her mother, name unknown, possible sounds like "Mee – Ann"
    - Olivia may have little brother, Stephen Roy, who has yet to have his abilities come in
        - Theory presented by *-redacted-*, a hypnotherapist who studies abduction phenomenon speculates that Dakota may have some grand purpose
    - This is prompted by the direct intervention of the archangel Michael and

possible ET parties to prevent Dakota from passing away

  ○ Another idea she suggested was that the reason certain entities take personal involvement with certain individuals is because of a likely ancestral relationship

    ■ If true, Dakota is a direct descendant of Michael the Archangel

      • Likely purpose of this, even if unintentional, may be so Michael can have vessels on this world capable of handling his essence without spontaneously combusting

      • Michael may also have a commanding role in the ET organization known as the Galatic Federation

-redacted-

• Was first to be attacked during the Hatman incidents

  ○ Wasn't present on panel but reached out to Dakota Frandsen via Whatsapp to

report a burning sensation on neck and that
he was coughing up blood
- Shows signs of having dealt with depression

-redacted-

- Suffered from depression due to bullying as
a child
    ○ Bullying instigated by his small stature
- Has tendency to take matters too seriously
- Protective of *-redacted-* due to brother/sister
dynamic
- *-redacted-* forwarded message from Brandon
with first line stating "CALL DAKOTA. I JUST
SAW OLIVIA"
    ○ *-redacted-* reported little girl appearing
    in his home just before a shadow apparition
    launched at him
    ○ "Shadow" then proceeded to compro-
    mise *-redacted-*, making him feel a deep
    sensation of dread when he would try to
    phone for help
        ■ Mentioned this feeling grew
        when Dakota's name was though of
        by Brandon

- *-redacted-*-forwarded messages to Dakota detailing the situation
  - *-redacted-* and Dakota proceeded to work their energies and respective deities to help Brandon severe the connection
    - The remote exorcism was possibly aided by Olivia
- While filming an episode of their podcast, "Ontario's Most Haunted" *-redacted-* both forwarded EVP clips of what sounded like a little girl
  - One clip sounded like "Ding dong"
  - Second clip was a clear "Mommy"
  - Dakota verified both clips sounded like Olivia
    - Speculation arose that this was Olivia's attempt to reach out to *-redacted-*
- *-redacted-* image was utilized in order to create the rendering of Olivia's face
- Without telling *-redacted-* entirely how the image was made, Dakota sent her the image to potentially identify a little girl she saw that she immediately recognized as Olivia

○ *-redacted-* gave a positive ID

• It is important to note that this DOES NOT guarantee-*redacted-* is in any way, shape, or form related to Olivia biologically

○ Two assumptions can be made knowing Dakota's family history

■ As Dakota is the only one of his siblings who doesn't need glasses, the potential for Olivia to have some sort of vision problems is high

• This indicates Ashley may have some physical resemblance to Olivia's biological mom

■ Assumption two is that Olivia was not traveling alone, being guided by her mother

-redacted-

• Has history of depression, suicidal thoughts, familial abuse, and substance abuse

• Reported some shadow beings, but nothing substantial enough to cause worry

-redacted-

• Has history of suicidal tendencies

- Is diagnosed with bipolar disorder
- Known pedophile
    - Working relationship terminated after incarceration
- Has had previous encounter with a potential demonic being tied to Aleister Crowley
    - Has mentioned that the encounter started when an audio tape of Crowley attempting to summon Satan
    - Shares that even though he ejected the tape, the audio kept going and the location started to shake
    - Though he speaks of it, it is obvious this encounter still bothers him
    - *-redacted-* has since declared Crowley to be a no-fly-zone to be handled by directors if something were to come up
- Worked in secret with Dakota to further research the Hatman phenomenon, even managed to locate a sketch of his true face

-redacted-

- Previous history of depression and suicidal thoughts

- Shows signs of minor mediumship ability
- Reported having car issues after the LOS attacks
  - Reported that one day, seemingly at random, a loud thud hit the top of his vehicle
  - For several weeks, car had issues with mechanics not being able to ID the source
- Might have been abducted by ETs
  - Believes to seen Olivia's mother on the moon

-redacted-

- Highly emotionally sensitive
- Reiki practioner
- Has had history of suicidal thoughts
- Tried conducting protection spells after Hatman attack
  - Reported signs of burning and choking
  - Shown photos of skin irritation
    - Symptoms went away after Danielle was advised to leave the case alone for the safety of her children
- Supported a known pedophile, possibly with romantic involvement

-redacted-

- History of foster care
- Dealt with some forms of abuse
- Supported a known pedophile
- Studied the LOS phenomenon extensively before joining *-redacted-*

-redacted-

- Recently joined *-redacted-* at the time of writing this report
- Has history of abuse and problems with illegal substances
- While on investigation in the Shoshone, Idaho he claimed he spotted the Hatman
    - Aside from uneasy feeling, he reported nothing happened afterward which could be connected
    - As of 08/19/2021 a deal was being discussed with city officials to help investigate locations in the area, which includes the local sheriff's office

-redacted-

- Psychic Medium
- Recent member of *-redacted-*

• While being interviewed for *-redacted-* was the one to point out to Dakota that Olivia may be half-Pleiadian

    ○ After the second interview, she validated that a computer generated rendering of Olivia's mother did in fact bare strong resemblance to a Pleiadian woman

    ○ In same interview *-redacted-* may have opened a door between members of *-redacted-*

-redacted-

- Possesses great psychic potential
○ Is unaware of how strong she may be
• Background in police dispatching
• Unknown if she ever had any run-ins with the Hatman but had interesting observations after watching three previous livestreams surrounding the February attacks

-redacted-

- *-redacted-* dedicated demonologist
- Shows great deal of knowledge in various fields
- In full honesty, it would be absolutely idiotic to not have his involvement for risky cases

Former -redacted- Members

-redacted-

- Possesses mediumship abilities
    - Offered Dakota Frandsen a mini-reading
        - Talked of Dakota being "particularly special" thanks to alleged connection to Michael the Archangel
        - During reading, EVPs came through of the being that could potentially be Dakota's daughter
        - After Dakota had a dream involving seeing an unidentified woman with his daughter Olivia, Victoria perked up as if she knew of the experience

- This is noted due to the fact, if genuinely some form of ET interaction, Dakota found his daughter and the unidentified woman in what appeared to be some kind of hospital room
    - Olivia tells Dakota, "Daddy, come meet my baby brother."
- History in psychology and law enforcement
- Was President of the company
    - Terminated due to leaking information and causing internal conflicts
    - Tried recruiting members from within to leave the company upon termination

-redacted-

- Registered Minister
- Had three near-death experiences
    - On a live, she discussed possibly being her own residual haunting
    - Reportedly at a former home she had an medical emergency which caused her to pass away briefly
        - She alleged the event can still be seen play out on location
- Claimed to have other "LOS" babysit her

after the attack to ensure we followed through on *-redacted-* word on walking away from the case

- This took place at the same time Texas had sudden freezing temperatures knock out many different facilities, including water and power, to many in the region
- Dakota Frandsen used spirit connections to strike "deal" with LOS, specifically addressing Cain
  - Walk away from all members of Parachills, and I will release a project that will allow him to torture even more people
- Plan was to buy time and use occult ties to build better defenses, potentially hurting the entity
  - Within hours *-redacted-* mentions the two of the "Hatmen" withdrew from her location
- *-redacted-* mentions they spoke in private about "the Knowing One," speculating that the entities were talking about me
- There is speculation surrounding *-redacted-*'s testimonies and contributions to these events
  - *-redacted-* is known to have pressured at least two men into attempting suicide

■ Progression of the suicidal spirals had escalated to the point of announcing to the public their intentions

○ *-redacted-* had also attempted staging a suicide attempt in order to get the attention of *-redacted-*

■ *-redacted-* claimed she had contacted paramedics

• In spite of being a self-proclaimed grammar Nazi *-redacted-* texted multiple people who were trying to talk her down in a manner that suggested she was inebriated

■ Dakota Frandsen notified authorities within her local jurisdiction

• Local dispatcher verified that no calls came from her location

■ After police left, *-redacted-* suddenly was in a clearer state of mind, verbally assaulting Dakota for "not trusting her" with perfect grammar

■ *-redacted-* was terminated from *-redacted-* shortly after

-redacted-

- Former Chief Operating Officer
- Claims to have connections to both Lilith and Lucifer
- History of drug use and domestic violence
- Possesses many of the same abilities as Dakota Frandsen
  - Upon taking the time to get to know one another it was discovered that *-redacted-* and Dakota came from nearly identical backgrounds in astrology, mental health, domestic violence situations, and even geographical history
  - As she was frequent in using methods of divination, as well as the Necrophonic app, *-redacted-* is also the first confirmed member of *-redacted-* to have been visited Olivia
- When stories of LOS were being collected by Parachills team members, *-redacted-* disclosed to Dakota directly that when she was about fourteen years of age she was attacked by a similar entity

○ She claimed to also have seen the LOS true face

    ■ Was shown the sketch of the Hatman's real face that was located by *-redacted-* validated it as the same one she noticed

• Dakota and *-redacted-* were able to use Necrophonics to send messages to one another

    ○ Numerous audio phenomenon was able to be captured by both parties, including catching each other's voices coming through a Necrophonic

• *-redacted-* and Dakota both participated in remote exorcism when *-redacted-* was attacked by a shadow entity in his own home

    ○ *-redacted-* believes that this incident was connected to an entity that identified itself as LOS in audio sessions

        ■ This entity had repeated to *-redacted-* several deragatory remarks as well through spirit box sessions

    ○ It should also be noted that the two involved were also able to hear each other's voices come through Necrophonic sessions at the same time

    ■ This was discovered by Dakota lining up both audio sessions upon the realization that both had coincidentally recorded overlapping sessions

-redacted-

- Quick temper
- Was terminated from *-redacted-* due to financial theft
- Has on and off cancer treatments
- 20+ years experience in the paranormal
- Was quickly caught off guard during the LOS attack during the livestream
  - While under the influence of the entity, whenever the name of Dakota Frandsen was
  mentioned he seemed to flinch
  - It was evident that the entity seemed to fear Dakota Frandsen
- When asked by Dakota Frandsen what he saw, *-redacted-* simply replied, "You already know."

Sherry Brett

- Practicing witch
  - Commits frauds frequently to gain notoriety
- Diagnosed borderline personality disorder
- Tries to claim that she was responsible for the LOS staying away from the team after the attack
- Violated company NDA and continues to try harassing *-redacted-* members
- Has established an illegal company practice in order to allegedly compete

T. C. Wilson

- Former marketing expert with *-redacted-*
- Left due to personal matters
- Was in relationship with *-redacted-*
- Encountered a rather violent attack from the LOS which he was saved by a man matching the description of Michael the archangel
- Talked of being able to astral travel, while in a sleep state, strongly enough to show physical ailments on his body

- ○ Example: if he were to travel to some-
where it was pouring rain or underwater,
he would
wake up soaking wet
  - ○ Swears up and down that sleep medi-
cation he takes makes it worse
- Claimed to have heard Dakota Frandsen's
name mentioned through the veil
- Believed Dakota to have physical connections
to a Christ bloodline
  - ○ Said that anytime Michael the archangel's name was mentioned there would
be a shine in
Dakota's eye
  - ○ When mention of Dakota came
through the veil, T.C believed Dakota had
connection to
Atlas
    - ■ Atlas is the name of one of the
stars in the Pleiades star cluster
    - ■ The Pleiades is speculated to
be where "Me – ann," the proposed
mother of Olivia, is
from
- Believed Dakota to somehow be connected to

visions of an apocalyptic event similar in nature to the one portrayed in the Nicholas Cage film, *"Knowing"*

-redacted- Contacts

-redacted-

- Practicing voodoo priest
- Was brought on to a live after the Hatman attacks where evident EVPs came through
    - A name was mentioned in the static was Dakota Frandsen
- Mike has evident attachments that seem to be of negative influence
    - Once Mike went into a trace state where he was triggered by Dakota Frandsen's presence
    - Mike mentioned that the entity seemed to fear Dakota
- Mike has a number of health issues which he believes firmly will cause the end of his life
- Owns property which he believes is stalked by a local Sasquatch tribe

Civilians

Cherry Mae

- Alias
- Dakota Frandsen's former investigation partner
- Had an abusive family situation growing up
which resulted in severe anger management issues
- Once told Dakota about seeing the Hatman
on top of a car
    - The person driving said car passed
    away later in the week
- As a teenager, Cherry once ran away from her
home to stay with what she refered to as her
"street family"
    - Strong indicators of stressors being
    related to her mother, as it was Mother's
    Day she
    decided to disappear
    - Upon hearing Dakota Frandsen was
    aiding in the effort to locate her, Cherry
    called her
    mother to be taken home
        - When asked, she said she knew
        if Dakota was to come to where she

was those she was

with would've been sent to the hos-

pital

- Reached out to Dakota out of desperation as she was suddenly attacked by the entity
  - The attack left her with three scratch marks on her shoulder
    - The shoulder was a tattoo of Dakota's name and a bear claw
- After an incident where Dakota was first possessed, Cherry got the tattoo for protection
  - The two were romantically involved

Tonya Arnold

- Alias
- Medium
- Was made known of Dakota by an online paranormal story podcast talking of his first encounters with his daughter
  - Had brief encounters with the Hatman as a teenager
  - Reached out to Dakota to say she had seen Olivia in her home state of Texas

- The encounter seemed random, as Tonya was just grocery shopping
- Was adamant that it was Olivia she saw because of how much she looked like Dakota
- Also claimed that Olivia was holding the hand of an unseen entity
  - Initial speculation pointed towards the invisible force was Michael the archangel
  - However the possible identity reveal of Olivia's mother renders the possibility that Olivia is being guided to Earth by her as highly likely
    - Tonya was shown the computer generated rendering of Olivia, the mother, and the possible younger brother
      - She recognized Olivia right away
      - She believed the mother was directly protected by Michael
      - She also remarked the younger brother has the same protections but has yet to grow into his abilities

Janet Dixon

- Alias
- Located in Georgia
- Had encountered the Hatman at a young age due to an abusive relationship
- Lives in a home she believes has potential demonic influence
    - Several violent crimes has taken place in the area
- Tried the use of a Necrophonic spirit box to communicate with her deceased brother
    - Reportedly claims she heard the phrase "Trust Dakota" come through

Damon Tripp

- Alias
- Father out of North Carolina mentioned earlier in report
- Relocated family from North Carolina to Idaho to escape activity
- Reached out to Dakota in regards to the activity
    - Claimed to been turned down by several group

- Discussed all the cliches of demonic possession
- Has used DMT in the past
    - Alterations to his mind may have passed on to his son, causing early signs of psychic ability
- LOS identified himself as Cain
    - LOS allegedly wanted to recruit Damon as some sort of leader role for in an army
    - Damon grew concerned as his young son seemed to be the center of LOS's focus after
the child turned three
- One particular room in the house was called the "Dead Room," by the wife
    - Feelings of dread, enough to cause physical sickness
    - Seemed to affect the men in the house more than the women
    - When discussing activty with Dakota, Damon happened to walk past that room
        - Disembodied voice of a small child, roughly aged six or seven, shouted "You hang up that phone or I'll fucking kill you."
        - This was the selling point for

Dakota to be convinced it was a genuine report

Emma Wright

- Alias
- Went to school with Dakota
- Upon discovering Dakota's knowledge of the paranormal Emma confided in him about activity she experienced
    - While only spooked by the LOS, she believes that something about his appearance drove
    her parents to split up

Tori Anderson

- Alias
- Dakota's fiance - deceased
- When she and Dakota met, Tori was pregnant and trying to escape her abusive ex
    - Had mentioned briefly that since her ex came into her life the Hatman had visited
        - Aside from uneasy feelings, no activity was to report

- ○ Tori was later murdered by the ex
  - ■ Baby did not survive
- ○ Tori's sister located Dakota online and read him entries from her diary
  - ■ The entries were more focused on how she prayed Dakota was being genuine with her

Harold Star

- Alias
- Contacted Dakota via Reddit to discuss details about the LOS
- Believed that LOS was repsonsible for the deaths of Harold's father and best friend
- Claimed the best friend left Harold a sword to attempt to kill the LOSwith
- Contact quickly dropped

Jane Christian

- Alias

- Dakota's ex
- Had history of sexual and physical abuse
- Seen the Hatman on several occasions
    - One such occasion she was locked into a bathroom while staying at a former boyfriends
    - The male subject claimed that the Hatman had appeared at said bathroom door, drew a
    knife, and charged at him
    - Needless to say the relationship didn't last
- Jane is diagnosed with borderline personality disorder due to her history of child abuse
    - Had toxic tendencies in relationships
        - Which involved serial cheating
    - Was exposed to her family after Dakota visited the area to confront suspicious activity in person
        - Jane responded by threatening Dakota with a restraining order

2024 Update

Addendum

The intelligence presented in this report encompasses various incidents up to the year 2021. Subsequent to this period, additional information relevant to this case has emerged, necessitating its disclosure as a moral imperative. However, it is crucial to note that mere recognition of the LOS and related phenomena could potentially expose individuals to danger. Consequently, this publication will contain guidelines designed to assist those who perceive themselves to be vulnerable. The aim of releasing this book is to ensure public transparency, and efforts will be made to distill the updated content into essential bullet points for brevity.

In Regards to the LORD OF SHADOWS (LOS)

- True Identity is Cain
  - Has been known by many names through various cultures
  - Cain was tempted by anger and resentment
  - Biological father, a being in the role of Samael, may have tempted Cain with a deal to embrace his "Mark"
  - The figure of "God" was likely Enlil from Sumerian mythology
    - Enlil has scouted several individuals from his half-brother Enki/Ea's creation/lineage in order to turn his creation against him
    - One such figure was Ea's son Marduk
    - Dakota Frandsen may have been offered a similar deal at the age of two, by both Enlil and Cain
  - Cain's new role served as an instrument of death, specifically targeting

individuals with high psychic potential as well as the capability to shed
familial blood

- Cain's role is likely the equivalent
of a high-ranking general in a literal
army of darkness, recruiting individuals who fit certain criteria to fulfill
various roles

  - Likely has monitored man-
  kind's progression and belief systems, taking inspiration
  from various mythologies all
  over the globe

    - This may be the in-
    spiration behind the bib-
    lical fourth horseman of
    the Christian apocalypse

  - Does not work alone, but
  ranks have since been slowly
  eradicated after the capture and
  imprisonment of Enlil

    - A few agents still re-
    main, all of likely human
    origins and are far less
    dangerous

In Regards to Dakota Frandsen

- Extraterrestrial Connections have been confirmed
  - Dakota fathered at least three hybrid children with a woman from a planet near Sirius B
    - Two girls and a boy
    - As of March 24th, 2024; the oldest two children are full grown adults
      - Dakota's oldest, Olivia, has a medical/scientific position within the Galactic Fderation of Worlds
        - Was recently married
      - Dakota's son, previously noted as "Stephen Roy," holds a position as a solider/pilot
      - Dakota's youngest, is still attending school
    - Mother of children specu-

lated to be envoy as well, possibly has been locatedc

- Dakota is speculated to be part of an extraterrestrial envoy program
    - Purpose of this program is to serve as an inside agent for a "Galactic Federation of Worlds"
    - Participation allowed Dakota to retain contact with extraterrestrial "family" to conduct operations involving supernatural threats on Earth
    - Participants of such programs are more popularly known in New Age circles as "starseeds"
- Dakota's physical bloodline has been traced, through geneological records and DNA testing, to be direct descendant of Ea
    - Bloodline also includes figures such as Adam and Eve, Cain, Yeshuah, etc...
    - The connections to figures

from religious and folkloric backgrounds have been confirmed by tracing known and DNA-backed royal ancestors of Dakota (such as Mary, Queen of Scots) through ancient records

- Dakota is likely from a planet near Alcyone, in the Pleiades Star Cluster
  - Dakota, known by a different name, was part of a rogue faction but defected to join the Galactic Federation of World
  - More in-depth information will be available in Dakota Frandsen's upcoming memoir "I Know You Won't Believe Me."

In Regards to Galactic Federation of Worlds

- Extraterresrial Military Organization
- Possibly originating from a point in 300 years relative to the Earth's future
- Comprised of various races allied together

to combat Invasive Greys and Draconian species

- Interacted with several individuals, all likely envoys, on Earth
    - Will explore envoy programs in further reading
- Exact details of operations are best detailed through works by Elena Danaan

Protection Sigil

Visualizing this image in your mind, replicating every detail, storing it on your electronic device, printing and carrying it with you, or incorporating it into your preferred protection practices can empower you against profound malevolence. Additionally, Dakota Frandsen has made a Protection Meditation available on all major digital music platforms, aiming to provide easy access to the audio for the wider public.

One can find the meditation on YouTube here: https://youtu.be/
iAO70ar8arI?si=nnbdrm3134vuAk99